SUPER SUNDAY
PLANNING EASTER FOR YOUR CHURCH

Edited by KEVIN D. HENDRICKS & ELIZABYTH LADWIG

Published by the Center for Church Communication
Los Angeles, California
www.CFCCLabs.org

Cover design by Laura Bennett.

"Easter, what?! Is it that time already?
Good grief this create-on-demand stuff is hard.
Let's just say a meeting is scheduled."

SHAWN WOOD

TABLE of CONTENTS

Foreword: Clear the Stage by Kelvin Co 1

PLANNING
Super Sunday Stats by Crystal Kirkman 6
The Best Easter Strategy: Stay Calm by Kelley Hartnett 9
Changing Your Church's Worship Schedule by Gerry True .. 13
Keeping the Easter Crowd by Evan Courtney 18
Lent: Offering More Than Hype by Angie Shoaf 22
Empowering Your Congregation to Invite Visitors
by Phil Bowdle 26

PROMOTION
24 Easter Ideas 31
Are Your Easter Service Times on Your Website?
by Kevin D. Hendricks 36
21 Ideas for Promoting Your Easter Services by Steve Fogg... 40
Easter Marketing Campaign: Found at Church
by Andrea Eiken 43
How to Welcome Easter Visitors by Kevin D. Hendricks 48
12 Last Minute Social Media Ideas
by Steve Fogg & Erin Williams 52

BEAT THE STRESS
3 Simple To-Dos for a Better Easter by Kevin D. Hendricks ... 60
You Recharge Your Phone, How About Your Soul?
by Adam Legg 64
Easter Is Over, Now What? by Kelvin Co 69
Scripture That Recharges the Soul by Erin Williams 73
An Easter Prayer for Church Communicators by Gerry True 75

MORE
About the Center for Church Communication 77
More Church Communication Help 79
Free Social Media Graphics 80
Acknowledgements 81

FOREWORD
Clear the Stage by Kelvin Co

After more than a decade of learning, shaping and molding, I've developed some pretty solid tried-and-true methods and go-to strategies for doing creative church ministry.

I've instilled a solid and clear God-breathed creative vision for our church, creative team and worship services.

Our series calendar has been consistently mapped out for an entire year. Major projects are planned months ahead, especially the "Super Bowl" of the church world—our Easter services.

I know how to do church communication.

But all that changed during Easter of 2013.

AN EASTER CHANGE

God did something amazing at my church, The Oaks Fellowship, and with our lead pastor, Scott Wilson. He talks about it in his book, *Clear the Stage*.

After months of planning, rehearsals, filming and promotions, we were rolling out the biggest Easter series we've ever done called "In Search of Oz."

Then God asked Pastor Scott, "Why are you doing this series? Did I tell you to do this?" God revealed to Scott that we had been doing a lot of cool and "godly" stuff and then asking God to bless it.

And yet, what God wants is for us to seek him first.

Before we plan, before we promote, before we launch this massive marketing strategy, God wants us to hear from him. God has a plan for our churches—one that's blessed and more successful than we can imagine—but we'll miss it if we don't stop and listen.

RESPONDING TO GOD'S CALL

Pastor Scott responded by ditching the messages he'd prepared for the series, which systematically dismantled the most creatively involved series my team has ever produced.

Each week we tore down the massive Emerald City set we built for the series in front of our congregation as a humble act of submission and obedience to the Lord as we surrendered our plans in place of his.

We scrapped the live re-enactment of scenes from the movie. In place of the musical productions that were to serve as live "bumpers" each week, Pastor Scott would humbly tell the congregation what we had planned and what God wanted us to say instead.

God was in fact asking my pastor to admit publicly that he was just a wizard behind the curtain. It was time to pull back the veil and show all our plans for what they were—nothing without God.

DESTROYING THE CALENDAR

Then, in complete and absolute obedience, Pastor Scott also blew up our entire series calendar for the year.

How we do programming and production planning for our services is now different. We will only do what we absolutely know the Holy Spirit clearly tells us. No more. No less.

Everything I knew about how to do my job was being thrown out the window—and I loved it!

FLEXIBILITY THROUGH GOD'S GRACE

God's grace enveloped me so thickly I embraced what was happening and was very excited. I knew it was going to be an uncomfortable process, but for the first time in my life I understood that I don't have to worry about anything because God is in control.

I am a planner—a very good one. It's easy for me to come up with strategies, solutions and creative ideas. But God wanted me to depend on him and teach me to "pray before I think." Romans 8:5 says, "Those who live according to the flesh have their minds set on what the flesh desires; but those who live in accordance with the Spirit have their minds set on what the Spirit desires."

I realized that I've been doing ministry according to what I think, want and desire. And that needed to shift and be Spirit-led.

PRAYING AND PLANNING

Easter continues to be the biggest service we prepare for. I still work on it months in advance. The level of creative production has not diminished.

The lesson here is not that God doesn't approve of big productions. There's nothing wrong with celebrating Easter—it's worth celebrating. The lesson is that as church communicators we need to seek God's plans for our churches first. We have to stop coming up with a plan and hoping God will bless it. We need to invite God into the process from the beginning and follow his lead.

Praying before I think—seeking his plans before I pursue what I think—is the coolest thing I can do. It's made my job more purposeful and easier. My life is the most fulfilling it's ever been.

So as you approach Easter this year, take a step back and listen for God's leading. Maybe he has a massive production in store for you, or maybe he wants you to scale it back and do something simple. Maybe God has a new liturgical direction, or maybe he's going to

3

speak freshly through what you've always done.

There's only one way to find out.

———————————

KELVIN CO gets to do what he loves as the creative arts pastor of The Oaks Fellowship located in the Dallas Metroplex area. Kelvin has been doing life together with his wife and best friend Lucy since 1991, and they have been doting on and pouring into their son Luc since 2002.

Web: KelvinCo.com | Twitter: @KelvinCo

PLANNING

SUPER SUNDAY STATS
by Crystal Kirkman

As we start thinking about planning Easter, it's important to understand the stakes.

It's pretty evident when you look at attendance patterns that guests are more likely to attend a worship service on Easter and Christmas.

LifeWay Research conducted a poll of 1,000 Protestant pastors asking for the three highest attended worship services throughout the year. The following holidays topped the list:

1. Easter (93%)
2. Christmas (84%)
3. Mother's Day (59%)

You can't deny the facts—Easter is the Super Bowl of the church. That means churches need to have their A-game in place before, during and after the event.

SEARCHING FOR EASTER ONLINE

Pew Research Center reported that more Americans search online for "church" around Easter than at any other time, with Christmas ranking second (Google Trends data between 2004 and 2013).

That means your church web presence is crucial to bringing in visitors at Easter. Make sure your website is welcoming and optimized for search engines.

EASTER INVITES

A personal invitation could make all the difference.

Don't assume that all self-identified Christians plan to attend Easter worship services.

Just two weeks before Easter, 20% of the individuals LifeWay Research sampled in another survey were still unsure if they would attend an Easter worship service. Imagine what a personal ask could accomplish with those who are unsure!

"Christians who automatically attend church on Easter should be mindful of their many friends, neighbors and family members who haven't ruled out the idea of attending," said Scott McConnell, director of LifeWay Research. "It may be that a personal invitation is what would make a difference to them."

RESOURCES FOR THE TIMID

It's vital to have a plan in place to make sure as many people as possible receive a personal invitation for Easter. The more resources you can provide to your congregation, the more comfortable and confident they will feel about asking someone to attend your Easter worship services.

Provide invitations that your church members can give to their acquaintances. Put together a media kit where people can invite others through their social media accounts. And of course, don't forget your own church media blitz.

CRYSTAL KIRKMAN is the communications director at First Christian Church in Decatur, Ill. She loves spending time with her husband, Tony, and their sons, Isaac and Christopher (Go Illini!).

Web: about.me/CrystalKirkman | Twitter: @ckirkman11

EASTER STORIES
Come As You Are

What's your favorite part about celebrating Easter at your church?

Bringing together the community by having our Easter service at a large auditorium located in our downtown area. We invite our community to 'come as you are,' and we even go to our homeless shelters to pick up the folks there by buses and take them to the Easter service.

Michelle Mumm is a graphic designer at King of Kings Church in Omaha, Neb.

THE BEST EASTER STRATEGY: STAY CALM
by Kelly Hartnett

Easter creeps up on us nearly every year, doesn't it? We're still patting ourselves on the back for surviving Christmas. Meanwhile, the Bunny's tiptoeing up behind us, ready to pelt us with Peeps (gross) and demand to see our brilliant Easter marketing plans.

Now, some of us—maybe four of us—handle this season with relatively little anxiety: calmly checking off to-dos, leaving plenty of time to make personalized, Pinterest-inspired gift baskets for everyone in the office. **Yeah, well, this chapter is for the rest of us.** The panicked ones. The I-can't-think-of-anything-creative ones.

Here's the best Easter marketing strategy I can offer: Calm down.

You still have time, and you can do this—especially when you remember it's not all up to you and your creative genius. You're not trying to dream up some wildly compelling story: the story's already there. When it comes to Easter marketing, your job is to pique curiosity. Granted, even that can feel a bit overwhelming, so let's approach it like you would tackle eating a giant, chocolate Easter bunny: one bite at a time.

BITE 1: SIT STILL AND LISTEN

When I'm stressed, my brain is of no use to me. None. It's a hummingbird that's flown into a garage; it's so freaked out that it can't see the solution—the gaping door—right in front of it. You can't expect to be at your creative best when you're hyperventilating. So stop. Breathe. Read the Easter story. Read it again. Flip through your file of amazing marketing pieces for inspiration. (Don't have one of those? Start one today.) Take in Stephen Brewster's blog—particularly the Graphic Design Inspiration posts he does on Mondays.

Caveat: While you're gleaning inspiration from other churches, ad agencies or wherever, *do not fall into the comparison pit.* That thing's like quicksand, and you'll find yourself suffocating in not-good-enough. Do the best you can with what you have.

BITE 2: START

I have a tendency to do all the easy stuff first—the stuff that ought to be waaaaaay down the priority list, but I do it first because it allows me to check off something and feel good about myself. That's not called productivity; that's called procrastination, and it's often rooted in a fear of failure. So just start. Brainstorm. Write it all down. Sketch it out. Just start.

BITE 3: COLLABORATE TO DEVELOP A PLAN

Even if you're a lone-ranger communication director/graphic designer/video producer/worship leader/youth pastor, this is not your project. Sure, you might care more about it than anyone else, but it doesn't belong to you. It belongs to your church. So share the chocolate bunny, for crying out loud, and make some decisions together:

- What's the theme of the worship experience?
- What creative elements can bring that theme to life?
- What marketing collateral might create curiosity?
- If you had limitless funds, what would you do, and what emotion would that evoke? Now, how can you accomplish that same thing within your budget?

BITE 4: CREATE ACTION ITEMS

Decide who's responsible for each element. Sit down with your calendar, assign deadlines, then back those deadlines up by a week so you have a bit of cushion. (It's the equivalent of setting your alarm 15 minutes early so you can hit the snooze twice. I don't know why it works, but it does.)

BITE 5: EXECUTE THE PLAN

Once the plan's set, don't start second-guessing yourself. Give yourself some credit, assume your head was clear when you put it together and make it happen. Plus, unless you skipped Bite 3, you've already had someone else look at it, and you've made any necessary adjustments, right? You're good to go.

BITE 6: EQUIP PEOPLE

Your church family is your marketing team. You might've developed an incredible, provocative direct marketing piece or Facebook ad that will pique the curiosity of the staunchest of skeptics. I love that. But skeptics are still more likely to accept an invitation from their neighbor than to respond to an impersonal advertisement. Think invite cards and shareable social media images.

Feel better? Yeah, me too. Now, if you'll excuse me, I'm going to pour myself a glass of milk, unwrap the bunny, and take the first bite.

KELLEY HARTNETT spent a decade working in established churches and helping to launch new ones. Currently, she's focused on writing, volunteering for organizations that care for vulnerable populations and making progress on her journey toward minimalism.

Web: KelleyHartnett.com | Twitter: @KelleyHartnett

EASTER STORIES
Keep It Simple

What's your favorite part about celebrating Easter at your church?

The fact that we show our true colors on Easter— not by going overboard on the program, but just by focusing on Jesus and doing what we usually do with extra excellence.

Mark Reiswig is the ministry catalyst at Catalyst Church in Phoenix.

CHANGING YOUR CHURCH'S WORSHIP SCHEDULE
by Jerry True

Easter is the summit of weekend worship services. It's the high point of the year (and of history) as we celebrate Christ's resurrection and his offer of eternal life. Such a defining moment and gracious gift deserves considerable celebration.

Preparing for a celebration of this magnitude takes substantial effort that should be more of a hike than a sprint. There's a mountaintop up there, but it takes work to get there.

Not long ago my wife and I hiked up Tom, Dick and Harry Mountain near Portland, Ore. As we entered the trailhead, a spry little lady—who appeared to be in her 70s—met us coming the other way. With a smile that betrayed a challenge, she inquired, "Are you going all the way to the top?" Well, if she had made it, we definitely would too!

That was a great idea. When we were at the trailhead, it was just friendly conversation and a nice ambition. We soon learned, though, that the hike was more than we bargained for—no matter the age of that lady. Our climb required a lot more effort than we had anticipated and a lot more water than we had packed. We questioned repeatedly whether we should turn back, but the lady's words resounded, and we would not be outdone.

THE EASTER MOUNTAINTOP

Planning for Easter reminds me of our hike. **We take up the**

challenge but are short on planning, resources and energy, so by the time Easter dawns, we are breathless rather than joyful. Planning the weekend service on a week-to-week basis—whether it is Easter or one of the other 51 weekends of the year—wears a team out and wears leaders down when we don't prepare well.

We all have 168 hours each week. The weekend service gets just one of those hours. That amounts to a minuscule one-half of one percent out of the whole week. This tiny number challenges us to become exceptional decision-makers and to choose carefully how we use the remaining hours to prepare.

Every Sunday leaders step up, speak up, and sing out to equip and inspire their people to walk with God. Our message is great and challenges us to give our best. We all want to get to the top of the mountain, and we have hundreds of worshippers who we want to take on the journey too. **So how do we get there without being empty ourselves?**

THE TIRED, OLD WAY

Six years ago our team lived in a familiar and frustrating blur, rushing from one week to the next to plan each worship service. We met on Tuesday mornings and left each meeting outfitted with overloaded to-do lists. We had four days left to carry out the decisions we had just made. Planning happened, but nothing was a sure thing. Every detail was open to change until the service began. Easter service was no exception. Each weekend service consumed so much time and energy that we had little left to re-ally consider what we actually hoped to create for Easter.

The burden and stress of this weekly cycle drove us to consider a better way. Our 70-minute time limit was immovable. We had to change. We knew we needed breathing room, so we found a better way.

THE BETTER APPROACH

We started planning several weeks in advance. Yes, easy to say, hard to do—at first. Since we were already breathless from planning just one weekend, planning more than one seemed like a daunting task. Yet today, neither our senior leaders nor our planning team would ever go back to the way it used to be. We all breathe easier and find that it's a good deal easier to reach the mountaintop (and enjoy it!) when we plan ahead. We found that our worship services (Easter included) improved when we created space to plan, prioritize and then implement the plan weeks in advance.

Instead of meeting weekly to talk only about the coming weekend, we set our sights several weekends out. **How did we do it? We started slowly.** We added one additional service to our weekly planning discussion. The meeting started by talking about the weekend that was two weeks away. The meeting ended with a recap of plans for the coming weekend service.

Working farther ahead also caused us to think about planning the Easter service in advance too. When you meet to plan your next service, why not commit to planning the following weekend too? Do that for a month; then add another week of planning to the discussion. Slowly repeat by adding just one weekend at a time to the discussion until several weeks are planned in advance.

Today, we plan seven weeks out year-round—except for Easter and Christmas planning. We begin planning these special celebrations three months in advance. Yes, three months.

COME PREPARED

Another thing we learned is that if everyone comes to the meeting ready to talk about the following weekend, decisions don't feel rushed. To do this, everyone comes to the meeting with their personal pre-planning completed. For instance, worship leaders select songs, create a road map and enter information into Planning Center for the weeks we will be discussing. Stage personalities (host, worship leader, etc.) are already selected, and assignments are made for who will handle transitions (welcome, communion, offering prayer, etc.). Anything planned outside of the meeting is handled and put into Planning Center Online. This provides greater opportunity for the most important things to be processed during our weekly meeting. Details are reviewed and tweaked. That's our weekly process.

Planning for big weekends like Easter begins with a special meeting. We explore creative ideas and settle on a theme and any creative elements we hope to include. The team leaves this meeting with assignments in hand—and it's three months before Easter. We hold a few additional meetings for Easter planning, and then Easter service discussions move into our weekly planning cycle. **The key is to initiate these conversations early so there is time to dream, pray and prepare.**

ENJOY THE VIEW

What would it feel like if you showed up to your Easter service fresh and ready for the mountaintop? I'm guessing you are like me. I would rather be left breathless by an amazing encounter with God than to be breathless from being empty and worn out. My wife and I started our climb up Tom, Dick and Harry Mountain thinking we were ready to scale the heights. Four hours later, we reached the summit to discover a stunning 360-degree view of five snowcapped volcanoes. The beauty was breathtaking, but the hike had been too, and we were spent. It didn't have to be that way if we had planned better. And it won't feel that way when it comes to Easter—or any other service—when we make time to prepare well so we can enjoy the view.

GERRY TRUE serves as the communication arts pastor at Oak Hills Church where he currently leads four teams of artists who use their creativity in communication, production, worship and technical arts. He lives in San Antonio, Texas, with his beautiful wife, Karen, and two delightful leaders-in-the-making kids.

Web: GerryTrue.com | Twitter: @GerryTrue

EASTER STORIES
Outdoor Services

What's your favorite part about celebrating Easter at your church?

This is the second year we will celebrate Easter with outdoor services. We are portable and currently meet in a movie theater, but for Easter we move our services outside into the shopping center. We've found it's a great way to let our community know we're there and invite them to join us. It has a very nostalgic vibe, which our people appreciate.

Carrie Evans is the communications director for Southbridge Fellowship in Raleigh, N.C.

KEEPING THE EASTER CROWD
by Evan Courtney

Easter services bring months of planning, special songs, kids singing on stage, helicopter egg drops, Easter Bunny photo booths and large crowds. Churches pull out all of the stops to proclaim the resurrection of their Lord and Savior.

Churches have record attendance on Easter and then return to normal the next week.

Why does that happen? We are the same church, with the same leadership, in the same location, with the same values. Where do all of these new people go, and why don't they return?

In Easter planning, an element that is too often forgotten is the week after. **We need to be sure we are pouring time, resources and energy into the weeks following Easter.**

FOUR WAYS TO GET GUESTS TO RETURN

1. Communicate the Upcoming Sermon Series
Churches spend a lot of money communicating their sermon titles and topics for Easter, but very little is spent on the next week.

Kick off your Easter message with a sermon series, and then communicate what you are teaching on the next week. Let visitors know what they are coming back to. Intrigue guests with next week's topic. Create anticipation.

2. Don't Let Your Congregation Slow Down
Most people come to church because of a personal invitation. A majority of first-time guests at Easter come through our doors because

someone invited them. That's awesome. But it needs to continue.

Encourage your congregation to continue to be bringers and braggers after Easter. That shouldn't stop. Your congregation needs to continue to bring their family, neighbors and friends they brought during Easter.

The goal is not just to attend an Easter service. It's to create life-long followers of Jesus.

Provide your congregation with tools and opportunities to brag about your church. Design social graphics they can easily share that talk up an amazing component of Easter at your church. Create quotes from the message, attendance numbers, numbers of those who received Christ, etc.

The social reach of your congregation is greater than their offline reach.

3. Develop a Good Assimilation Process
We've prayed, planned and gotten people through the doors. Now what? Create a process to make your church 'sticky' for guests.

Communicate one action step you want a guest to take after attending Easter. It's easy to overload them with content about all your available ministries, a full welcome packet or asking them to sign up for one of a hundred classes.

But that can be overwhelming. What's one, simple action step they can take?

I think it should be to attend next week. That's it. Nothing else. Just come back next week.

Now you need to develop an assimilation process around that action step. It could include giving guests a gift to help them remember your church, sending emails inviting them back next week or a phone call asking how their experience was.

4. Speak the Language of Your Guest
If you want guests to come back, they need to feel welcome.

That's going to require going the extra mile to speak their language. I'm not saying that if guests cuss, your church leaders should cuss. Just don't use words guests don't know or understand. Put on a filter and walk through your Sunday morning experience with the eyes and ears of a first-time guest. Here are some things to consider:

- Everyone who speaks on the stage, including the lead pastor, should introduce themselves by name. Don't assume everyone knows who they are.
- Screen pre-service graphics specifically for guests. Provide them with information about kids' ministry check-in, bathroom locations, whether or not they can bring a drink in the auditorium, etc.
- Let them know what to expect during the service. Use an emcee to explain what happens during the service and how long it will take. This can be as simple as, "It's great to have you at First Church today. This morning, our team will lead us in a couple of songs, and then the pastor is going to give us an inspiring and challenging message."
- If you're a liturgical church and an emcee or host doesn't fit, then use liturgy that clearly explains what's about to happen or make sure details of what to expect are spelled out in the bulletin.

KEEP THEM COMING BACK

Easter is a great opportunity to attract new guests to our churches each year. But that opportunity is wasted if we don't find ways to keep them coming back to church during the rest of the year.

Find ways to connect with guests and make them feel welcome during Easter services. If you do, they might just become regular attendees and begin cultivating a relationship with Jesus Christ.

After all, that's the primary goal.

EVAN COURTNEY is an executive pastor in the middle of the Illinois cornfields at The Fields Church. He owns a creative design company, Creative Courtney, and is a Creative Missions alumni.

Web: EvanCourtney.com | Twitter: @EvanCourtney

EASTER STORIES
Unity

What's your favorite part about celebrating Easter at your church?

The focus on the central reality of the death and resurrection of Jesus Christ. It is this central truth that brings unity across the wide diversity of our church.

Santosh Ninan is a pastor at
Bethel Grove Bible Church in Ithaca, N.Y.

LENT: OFFERING MORE THAN HYPE
by Angie Shoaf

Typical marketing excels at hype. You recognize the increasing levels of promotion and busyness that can reach a fever pitch. But the church has another way. Instead of hype and frenzy leading up to Easter, the church has penitence.

Whether your church is liturgical or not, the time known as Lent—the 40 days before Easter—can bring an opportunity for a particular type of depth to worship not found at other times of the year. It is a time of penitence and reflection, of seeing the suffering of Christ.

Traditionally, Lent has been a season of sacrifice when Christians throughout history have given something up as a way of experiencing in some tiny way the sacrifice of Christ. But no matter where your church lands in the denominational spectrum, Lent is an opportunity to help your congregation draw closer to Christ and deepen their faith as we approach Easter.

It all begins with Ash Wednesday, the first day of Lent (or maybe Fat Tuesday and a pancake supper for you traditionalists). Ash Wednesday is observed with an evening service in many churches where ashes (often from the burned palm branches of the previous Palm Sunday—again, for you traditionalists) are used to mark a cross on the forehead of believers to remind them both of their baptism and of the fleeting nature of life. This is a service for beautiful and solemn music, deeply meaningful art and silence. Ash Wednesday is full of thoughtfulness about the journey of the next 40 days of Lent leading toward Christ's suffering and death.

THE THEME OF LENT

People today see suffering the world over, whether it's on their favorite media outlet or on Twitter, Facebook and Instagram. And they also see their own suffering from causes that can be obvious to all or invisible to most. These are the members of your church and the community you hope to serve, and in any given year at least a portion of them will be going through intense personal suffering.

The job of the church communicator is to show everyone you reach that the church is where God can reach them, and they can reach God. It's a place to bring them from suffering to joy through fellowship with fellow believers and ultimately, through fellowship with God.

Lent is a time of drawing people into the church, to bring people together to see their collective journey. It's an opportunity to acknowledge the pain and suffering of this world and to point to the hope that Christ both knows our suffering and has overcome it.

Lent can be a thematic build-up to Easter that connects with people much better than hype. There are some evocative ways to use communication to enhance how people connect with Lent. Whether your church has weekly soup suppers, simple meals or a special series of Bible studies, create opportunities for people to connect with the themes of Lent and help them prepare for Easter.

Here are a few ways you can explore Lent in different mediums:

ART:

- Create artwork paired with a verse or Bible story to enhance the week's discussion of that point in the journey. It could be classic artwork you find online or something original, either created by a local artist or some artistic children in your community.
- Turn a portion of your space into an art display for Lent to focus on this season and be a catalyst for discussion.

- Explore the Stations of the Cross in art, either through the Lenten season or for a special service or gathering. This is especially powerful during Holy Week leading up to Easter.

MUSIC:

- Each week post a piece of music or a video with music focused on a Lenten or current world topic that provokes thoughtfulness on the suffering world through a Christian perspective. Highlight your church's missions ministry or the work your church is doing to come alongside suffering people in your own neighborhood or around the world.
- Hold a concert or a series of concerts to fundraise for those in need and enjoy music that is born of suffering. This could be global music, blues, classical or some other genre based on the knowledge and interests of your church's musicians.
- In your weekly church communication, highlight a song or hymn from the Sunday service and give a bit of the story behind it, whether it is on the song or the life of the composer.

SERVICE:

- Communicate what your church is doing to serve through Lent, whether it's your local soup kitchen or shelter, your men's, women's or youth group's work, or other missions.
- Run a single appeal for all of Lent with a measurable goal for a service project where your church comes alongside a group that is suffering and helps to shoulder the burden, whether it's fundraising for a local group in need or lobbying for a change in policy to help the poor, the hungry or the outcast.
- In your communication, highlight a different outreach being coordinated by your greater church body each week. This could be global emergency response work, food for the poor, medical outreach, etc.

Lent can be an opportunity to focus your congregation in anticipation of Easter and do so much more than simply promote your Easter services. Don't let the weeks leading up to Easter be full of suffering as you struggle for greater heights of hype. Instead, make it a time of solidarity with the suffering, to show that Christ understands suffering, and to learn what God does about suffering through the hands and hearts of his people. It will make the promise of Easter shine that much brighter.

———————

ANGIE SHOAF wears a few hats around Christ on Capitol Hill in Saint Paul, Minn., from office staff to communications strategist to events coordinator. Her interests range from art and photography to literature, travel, and keeping up with the latest developments in tech and the sciences.

Facebook: /Angie.Shoaf.14

EASTER STORIES
Lillies & Lent

What's your favorite part about celebrating Easter at your church?

Each year our congregation is able to memorialize a loved one by donating an Easter lily to decorate the sanctuary. We list the loved ones' names in our bulletin to make it extra special for everyone. I enjoy that tradition and how it ties in with the resurrection.

Jennifer Johnson is the director of communications for Sewickley Presbyterian Church in Sewickley, Penn.

EMPOWERING YOUR CONGREGATION TO INVITE VISITORS
by Phil Bowdle

I've got good news and bad news.

Whether you're a pastor, communications director or ministry leader, you have a role to play when it comes to marketing.

Marketing doesn't have to be an ugly or secular word. In a church context, it's simply sharing opportunities for your church and community to engage in.

For years, churches have jumped to conventional methods to promote what they have going on at their church. Many focus on things like bulletins, stage or pulpit announcements, brochures and emails. Others have the budget to utilize more expensive methods like newspaper ads and billboards.

Here's the bad news.

These conventional marketing methods are growing less and less effective. Your audience has more messages and clutter competing for their attention than ever before. It's becoming increasingly difficult to get noticed in a noisy world. Emails are only opened on average between 20-30% of the time. Bulletins are getting thrown away. Stage or pulpit announcements are only reaching the segment of your audience that shows up that day (the average person typically comes to church only once or twice a month).

Printing has become more expensive and is being replaced by a digitally driven culture. Some churches may be finding success in a few of these areas, but for the majority these traditional efforts are simply not getting the job done.

Here's the good news.

There is a method that is typically overlooked and many have forgotten. It also happens to be the least expensive and most effective way to spread the word about what your church is doing for Easter (or any Sunday for that matter).

WORD-OF-MOUTH MARKETING

Our greatest influencer on what you watch, read, attend or participate in is the recommendation of friends and family.

Most of us would say that we're aware of the power of word-of-mouth marketing. The problem, though, is that so few are changing their communications strategy to equip their audience to do this effectively.

So what if we could look beyond what we've always done and look for ways to tap into the most effective marketing tool at our disposal—our congregation?

Here are some practical tips to equip your congregation to be your most effective marketing tool:

Tip #1: Share a Compelling Vision or Goal

Empower your audience with a compelling vision and goal they can be part of. This can't come across as a "we can do it, you can help" message. Help your audience join in the story you're telling at Easter this year by sharing a compelling vision they want to see happen and embrace the Home Depot model of "You can do it, we can help!"

Your audience wants to be a part of something bigger than themselves. Don't just settle for sharing your vision. Invite them into your vision. Give them a clear call to action and share with them how they can be part of making it happen.

Tip #2: Give a Clear Call to Action

With every message, clarify what your intended response is. Give your audience a simple call to action so they know what their next step should be. Make it clear and compelling, and remove any barriers that could cloud that message.

Tip #3: Use the Power of Social Media

Our culture has become a sharing culture. Through social media, we naturally have an audience of friends and family we can share with at the click of a button. Because of this, social media has become a game-changer in marketing and can help your message spread farther, faster. What does that mean for us? It means we have to stop using social media as a bullhorn for our information. We need to start creating content that works natively for social media that your audience would want to share.

The content you create for a service may not translate well on social media. Some of the most effective communication we have done with my team at West Ridge Church is by filtering social media content around the question of "Would I want to share this with my network of friends?" If the answer is no, change the strategy.

Tip #4: Equip Your Audience With a Tool to Start a Conversation

Yard signs, invite cards, door hangers and social media posts can all resource your audience to engage their friends and family. It's not the tool that makes this effective. It's the conversation your congregation has that makes this powerful. You're just providing the information they need to help them take their next step.

Tip #5: Make Your Content Easy to Share

Add share buttons on your website so people can share the information on their social media platforms or by email. Make your tweets shorter so people can re-tweet and add comments to their post. Create images your audience could use on their own profiles to help promote and tell the story of what you're doing at Easter.

EMBRACE THE REALITY

The reality of promoting your Easter services is that your communication team can only do so much. But you can multiply your efforts by empowering your congregation.

PHIL BOWDLE is the creative arts pastor at West Ridge Church in Atlanta. Follow along with his blog at PhilBowdle.com for practical systems and resources for the creative church.

Web: PhilBowdle.com | Twitter: @PhilBowdle

EASTER STORIES
For the First Time

What's your favorite part about celebrating Easter at your church?

Welcoming thousands into our home! Sharing the love and grace of Jesus in unexpected ways. Knowing that people will encounter and experience the presence of God—sometimes for the very first time!

Christine Pitt is the communication/creative director at Valley Creek Church in Flower Mound, Texas.

PROMOTION

24 EASTER IDEAS

What does your church do for Easter? Sometimes it helps to hear stories from different churches and be inspired by something new and different. We've collected stories of what churches have done for Easter over the years. Some of it might fit into your planning or work better for promotion. Not every idea will work in every church, but check out the list and see if you can find some inspiration.

1. Sunrise With a View: The congregation I attended as a child did a sunrise service on the lawn of a museum outside of the airport in my hometown. The kicker was that the airport and the museum are on top of a plateau about 200 feet above the main town making for beautiful views of God's creation. -Carrie Gubsch

2. Crashing Cross: Kelvin Co and the creative team at The Oaks Fellowship in Dallas put together a powerful video that tells the testimony of Bill Bair and ends with a cross crashing to the ground.

3. All About the Kids: At Easter we always have our kids do speeches and skits/plays. We find that even those who don't regularly come to services like to see their kids or other kids perform. We almost always give out small snack bags to all in attendance. -Cynthia Chandler

4. Dance, Dance, Yeah: Modern dance interpretation of The Passion, performed by a teenage girl! -Terra Osterling

5. Easter Rap: You want original Easter ideas? Try a rap video courtesy of Hingepoint Church in Bakersfield, Calif.

6. Interfaith: We have a joint Passover Seder and Easter dinner to celebrate the commonalities of faiths, rather than the differences. We participate in an Interfaith Hospitality Network in which churches, synagogues and even secular humanist groups work together to provide housing to families who have lost theirs. -Win Morgan

7. Week Early: We hold services the week before so members can still go to a really amazing Easter service and be with their families on the actual holiday. -Sarah Myers

8. Good Friday Baptisms: On Good Friday, a church I was on staff with placed an above-ground pool in the middle of the sanctuary and baptized about 80 people. We surrounded the pool with our regular chairs so families and friends could watch their loved ones surrender their lives wholly to Christ. -Tanya Glass

9. Cardboard Testimonies: We did a series of six stories of changed lives with a very short phrase written on cardboard and a photo of the person/people holding the sign in the weeks leading up to Easter. We built a wooden cross with 2x8s that was open on the inside, put magnets on the outward facing edge, covered the cross with brown craft paper, and then put magnets on the back of the six cardboard signs that had been used in the photos. As the pastor spoke about each thing that people had been saved from, he removed the sign from the cross. Eventually, there was an empty cross, signifying that on Easter, the cross was empty. There were brown papers with commitment boxes to check under each seat. We tore the paper roughly to look like mini cardboard testimony signs. People were invited to write what they had been saved from on the back of the paper and bring it to the foot of the cross. -Priscilla Hammond

10. Art Show: Our arts ministry—IMAGO—hosts an annual Holy Week art show beginning two weeks before Easter Sunday with pieces submitted by professional and amateur artists within the church family. Each year's theme either points to Easter specifically or is tied to the pastor's message series from the previous year. With some members being well-known in the local arts community, the art show has drawn people to the church who may otherwise never have come. -Steven Murray

11. Fireworks Video: C4 Church in Ajax, Ontario, Canada, constructed a 14-foot cross out of wood and string with different sins written on it. If you think you've seen this before, wait for the words to start flying off and the fireworks to start. It's a great video about sin and redemption.

12. The Choice: We did a cool presentation of a dramatized and musical message we called "The Choice." It was set on a park bench with a lamppost that also served as a directional signpost at which different people's stories intersected. Eventually, all their stories intersect and the subtle message at the end is that life is meaningless without an authentic relationship with Jesus. There was a standing ovation at the end of the production as well as an unbelievable response to the altar call. -Joseph Thompson

13. Edible Eggs: One church gave out decorated, edible eggs to homeless/needy individuals with short messages on them such as "Jesus Died 4 U." -Steven Proctor

14. Repeat Eggs: Long Hollow Baptist Church in Henderson-ville, Tenn., put Easter eggs stuffed with a bouncy ball and an invitation on everyone's front door in the neighborhood of their church. But it didn't stop there. They did it again a couple of days later with a second egg in their front yards. A local blogger was on the receiving end and posted about it: 5 Marketing Lessons from a Hipster Church.

15. Picture Time: One church took studio-quality pictures of families and then delivered real photo portraits. -James Brown

16. Photo Booth: Last year my church did a photo booth in conjunction with Easter. We figured Easter was the big day to dress up and thought people would want something free to commemorate the day. So we set up a photo canvas, incorporated some props to add some fun elements (including live baby chicks) and had a great time. We actually doubled our attendance for the day. -Jon Rogers

17. Selfie Banner: Stone Creek Church in Urbana, Ill., created a banner that had Easter branding and service times on it and encouraged people to take selfies with it. They also shot a music video for Pharrell Williams' "Happy" and posted on it on social media channels to promote their Easter services.

18. Service Before Service: Our church serves food before the services to our community, drawing many homeless and needy people.
-Tracielynn Raterman

19. LED Jesus: Rockford First in Rockford, Ill., created freestanding letters (spelling Jesus) outlined with DMX-controlled LED lighting. To accomplish this they used plywood, Coroplast and LED tape.

20. Light It Up: Last year, our church got theater lights to highlight the altar. It sounds cheesy, but it ended up being beautiful.
-Sarah Boyette

21. Triple Wide Creation: The Orchard Community in Aurora, Ill., put together two triple-wide setups (six projectors total) and projected on white parts of their side walls and masked their brick "pillars," which gave it a window effect. They introduced this environmental projection during the creation story in their Easter services.

22. Passion Play: I went to a church where they acted out the Easter story. They had rented a large auditorium for Easter and had incredible sets. It really made an impact. -Leslie Zander

23. Shareable Graphics: The Fields Church in Mattoon, Ill., created a series of shareable Facebook graphics that targeted different elements of their Easter services. They also designed a specific invitational marketing piece they put into the hands of elementary-aged kids so they could invite their school friends.

24. Alleluia, Alleluia: For me, the coolest thing about Easter is the celebration. With the triumphant music, the crowd and the palpable joy in the air—it makes church feel like a party. Then there's the anticipation. In a liturgical church like mine, every service ends with the congregation responding to our pastor's exhortation with, "Thanks be to God, Alleluia, Alleluia." Except during Lent when we simply say "Thanks be to God," (that first week someone inevitably forgets). For six weeks we haven't said "Alleluia" to close the service, and at Easter we let loose and shout out with joy: "Alleluia, Alleluia!" It sounds like a ridiculous overstatement, but it really feels like heaven.

-Kevin D. Hendricks

EASTER STORIES
Farmers Market

Share one cool way your church is spreading the word about Easter this year:

Our theme was centered on the part in Scripture where Mary had mistaken our Lord for a gardener. So we had a gardener theme, and our invites were packages of seeds to plant. We had tomato, cucumber and carrot packets to hand out. On the front of the packet was an invite to our service.

We also had pop-up farmers markets at local parks where we were able to hand out bags of free, fresh local produce. Inside the bags were also the seed packet invites. On the packet was a website we created for our Easter service. It had all the information of the Easter service, the location and a map to get there for our guests. It had links to other sites such as our web page, Facebook page, and our locations and times of our farmers markets.

We spread the word about these markets through social media and word of mouth through our congregation. We also printed up large yard signs to put out on the main streets to the parks.

Michelle Mumm is a graphic designer at King of Kings Church in Omaha, Neb.

ARE YOUR EASTER SERVICE TIMES ON YOUR WEBSITE?

by Kevin D. Hendricks

When Easter rolls around, a lot of churches with communication teams are all-hands-on-deck. Everyone is busy making final preparations, tweaking production and rolling out social media elements. Your print pieces are already done. It's a lot of work, but you're getting there.

Then there are the churches that don't have a communication team. You don't do fancy sermon graphics or a giant production. Oh, you'll bust out the choir robes on Easter Sunday and have a production, but it won't involve a projector and mood lighting.

These are churches like mine. And for these churches I have a simple, yet powerful Easter idea: **Put your Easter service times on your website.**

We already know that more people will visit your church on Easter than any other Sunday of the year. **But how can they visit if they don't know when your Easter services are?**

WELCOME THE VISITORS

This seems brain-dead obvious. But somehow we overlook it. We assume people will figure it out. Or your Easter service times are the same as every other Sunday, so there's no need, right? Wrong. **People thinking about coming to your church for Easter are likely a little nervous and unsure of what they're doing.** You want them to feel welcomed, to know they're going to the right place at the right time. If they visit your website and there's not a word about Easter, you're just stoking that anxiety. But if they see Easter mentioned, they'll feel welcomed and reaffirmed.

It's such a tiny thing, but it can make a big difference. Especially if you're doing something different. If you've got an extra service, different times or something special, you must let people know.

We've written an entire book about welcoming visitors and have tons of resources. Get in their shoes, especially at Easter, and help them feel welcome.

EASTER SURVEY

I did a quick experiment with a Google search for "church" in my area. I checked out the area churches less than 20 days before Easter and found that only nine out of 20 churches had Easter info on the front page. Now granted, a lot of these are smaller neighborhood churches. Not a megachurch in the bunch. They likely don't have a communication team.

But this isn't a case where the tech-savvy churches automatically had their Easter info up. Some had slick, new websites without a mention of Easter. Others had pretty woeful websites that still had Easter info. **What matters here is actually updating that site.** A lot of them could easily slap some text on the homepage with Easter service times. Or put a quick graphic in the slider.

(And megachurches? I checked a few, and three out of four had Easter info on the front page. So maybe some bigger churches need a reminder too.)

PUT EASTER ON YOUR SITE

Those big churches (most of them anyway) have had their Easter graphics splashed across their website for a few weeks now. Good for them. We may covet their quality design, but we can borrow this simple idea of putting the info out there.

Here are a few tips on how to do it right and lessons from my Google searching:

- **Put Easter info on the front page.** Don't make potential guests hunt for it. Don't think your newsletter or events calendar is good enough. One church had a kids' Easter celebration mentioned in their newsletter. But how many people will dig that deep? Home page, people.
- **It's OK to link deeper for more details.** Many of us don't have a lot of flexibility on our website, and it can be hard to squeeze in new stuff (and it's a good way to clutter up your design). One church simply had a "Holy Week Schedule" link. It wasn't flashy and it linked to a PDF (ug), but it's better than nothing.
- **Make sure it's actually linked.** Test it. One church site I visited had a slick graphic in their homepage slider. Nicely done. But the graphic had no details and when I clicked, it didn't go anywhere. Fail. Other graphics in the slider were linked, but not this one. That's either an oversight (test it!), or it's useless.
- **Above the fold.** Ideally your Easter info should be above the fold. One church had it all the way at the bottom. Good job for getting it out there, and maybe that's the only place they could put it. But that's expecting a lot out of your visitors.
- **More than a calendar.** One church had their Easter info in an automatic calendar in the sidebar. They had the date and the time, which is better than nothing. But clicking through didn't give any extra details. This is an opportunity to invite people to your Easter service. Take that opportunity and at least give them something. You could always link to your general visitor page (you have one, right?) to answer basic questions. Or link to your contact page and invite them to ask questions.
- Get social. Now is also the time to start talking about Easter on social media.

GO DO IT

So whether your church is big or small, fancy website or something basic, communication team or solo volunteer, Easter plan or seat of your pants—**go put your Easter service times on your website!**

KEVIN D. HENDRICKS is the editor of Church Marketing Sucks and editorial director for the Center for Church Communication. He's a freelance writer and editor in St. Paul, Minn., and likes to read a lot—he wrote *137 Books in One Year: How to Fall in Love With Reading.*

Web: KevinDHendricks.com | Twitter: @KevinHendricks

EASTER STORIES
Microsite

Share one cool way your church is spreading the word about Easter this year:

This year, we launched a one-page microsite on a subdomain of our website. All of our communication channels (platform, print, social, advertising, etc.) point to that domain. This was a 'test the waters' sort of thing while our new site was being developed. I wanted potential guests to have a better first impression of our church than our existing site could provide. Publishing a one-page WordPress theme was the quickest way I could conceive of achieving that.

Jared Brandon is the director of communications at Parker Hill Church in Scranton, Pa.

21 IDEAS FOR PROMOTING YOUR EASTER SERVICES
by Steve Fogg

Our weekly #cmschat on Twitter invited participants to share their tips and ideas for promoting Easter services. It created an opportunity to cover a number of communication channels and get input from a range of different churches.

Here are some of those tips and ideas. You will notice they are short and sweet as we were, after all, on Twitter.

IN SERVICES/AT CHURCH

- Frequently remind your congregation to invite friends and family during the lead up to Easter.
- Give them the tools (e.g., invites) to take away so they don't forget to invite friends.
- Do it early and often. Do it actively and passively.
- Use storytelling to promote the why, not just the what.
- Make the purpose of your Easter service obvious—evangelism. Audiences will connect with the purpose behind the service and it will motivate them to invite their friends.
- Create visual marketing through posters (in foyer) as well as video trailers.
- Use a short drama/skit on stage to engage the idea.
- Mail out postcards to the community, as well as the personal invite.

SOCIAL MEDIA

- Create an organic Easter video on Facebook as the reach explodes.
- Create a photo booth as a social invite that people can

- share from the Facebook page and tag their friends.
- Start an Instagram competition to encourage others to repost a picture and tag 10 friends they would like to invite and win something.
- Make sure you use photos or videos as these have a higher engagement than plain text.
- Do an Easter photo countdown challenge where people have to take a photo and use a unique hashtag.
- Create a landing page with graphics for people to share from a central point (NewSpring has a generic social media kit). Also, email the link to your congregation.

EMAIL

- Use email to boost your key Easter social media posts. Invite your congregation to share the post with those they want to invite.
- Keep the emails short and direct to the message.
- Create personal email e-vites (Harvest & Eagle Brook churches have good examples).
- Create a squeeze page to build an email list.

OUTDOOR/RADIO/PR

- Create a large banner for the church building. Let the building become the billboard!
- If you do a drama, offer media interviews with the local cast. Local papers love those stories. It's a great way to authentically reaching your audience without being pushy.
- Consider movie theater advertisements.

Thanks to everyone who participated in the #cmschat for sharing their ideas and inspiration.

———————

STEVE FOGG serves as the big cheese of communications at his church in Melbourne, Australia; he married way above his pay grade and has three children. Connect with him on his blog or on other social networks.

Web: SteveFogg.com | Twitter: @SteveFogg

EASTER STORIES
Content

Share one cool way your church is spreading the word about Easter this year:

We've been trying to fill our blog with valuable content: blog posts about why we do the traditions we do, posts about people/stories, etc. (e.g., holy week explained, blessing of the baskets, tips for inviting someone).

Tom Lelyo is the director of youth and young adult outreach at St. Thomas More Catholic Church in Sarasota, Fla.

EASTER MARKETING CAMPAIGN: FOUND AT CHURCH

by Andrea Eiken

Like most churches, we typically do some external advertising around Easter. But as our staff sat around a table talking about how to reach our target audience, we realized something pretty key.

Most people already know that Easter is coming. We're a church. No one needs us to let them know we're having Easter services. It's the world's biggest no-brainer.

Here's where we started:

AUDIENCE

The somewhat-churched, the open-to-church, the desperate seekers, the two-timers (Easter and Christmas), the casual churchgoers. Anyone who is a little bit familiar with Christianity and what this time of year means.

DEMOGRAPHICS

25-55 years old. Male and female. Culturally diverse. Tech-savvy. Baby Busters (1965-1980), Gen X (1975-1985), Gen Y/Millennials (1978-1990). Suburban and first-ring urban commuters. Public-transit users.

METHOD

Focus on public transportation advertising opportunities. Engage current attenders in an invitation initiative that aligns with external ads and will continue past the Easter season.

Create a website (foundatchurch.com) that generates content from attenders' social media engagement with a specific hashtag (#foundatchurch). External ads promote the website.

WHAT HAVE YOU FOUND AT CHURCH?

So instead of blabbing on billboards and direct mail pieces about how fantastic our Easter services would be, we made the decision to simply ask people who've experienced God change their life through attending church to tell others: **What have you found at church?**

Our graphic designer Kellie Cornell designed an incredible range of ads for us to use on social media and in external channels.

We launched with a video and caption on Instagram and Facebook:

> What have you found at church? Wisdom? Friendship? Acceptance? Whatever you've found, post it from your Facebook, Twitter or Instagram accounts using #foundatchurch. Your stories tell the stories of Eagle Brook Church and show others what they can find here, too!

> Throughout the month of March, your #foundatchurch posts will show up at foundatchurch.com. Take a look, share your story and, together, let's tell others of Jesus' incredible love.

The following weekend, we passed out invite cards after services at every campus and aired a video before services explaining the campaign.

THE REACTION

During the first week, **attenders started posting what they had found at church**, and we saw great engagement. It was very exciting to watch it take off!

In recent years, **we have seen great return on investment when advertising through public transit channels**. People love seeing their church out in the community, interacting with people from all walks of life.

Attenders often take photos of Eagle Brook Church (EBC) ads on buses and share them on Instagram, Twitter and Facebook. It's been a great way to get attenders to talk about their church within their social media communities.

HOW TO TARGET YOUR MESSAGE

For these reasons, **we decided to focus more heavily than we previously have on targeting suburban and first-ring urban commuters** with this campaign.

By targeting suburban and first-ring urban commuters who utilize public transit, we have the unique ability to specifically speak to people who live near our campuses **without using direct mail or digital billboards.**

Direct mail has historically proven to have a very poor ROI and digital billboards can be very expensive with possibly low impressions depending on preferred ad space availability.

Buses with EBC advertisements were specifically assigned to run from transit center garages through our campus communities, through both downtown Minneapolis and St. Paul, back to suburban park-and-rides and neighborhood stops.

Riders become familiar with the ads as they see them repeatedly for five weeks on their buses. Pedestrians, many of whom are suburban car-commuters, become familiar with the ads as buses pass by downtown.

Those waiting at bus shelters will become familiar with poster ads, connecting them visually with the bus tails and the interior bus ads. Ten transit shelter ads also rotated throughout downtown Minneapolis over the course of the four weeks leading up to Easter.

HOW TO FOCUS YOUR MESSAGE

Additionally, we made the strategic decision to not give ourselves away completely in the design of these ads. **We wanted the stories to speak more loudly than our name.**

So on all of the bus shelter ads, we used the foundatchurch.com URL vs. eaglebrookchurch.com. We were required to include Eagle Brook Church on the bus tail and interior ads for legal reasons, but we were allowed to keep it small so it didn't distract from the core message of the ads.

Our hope is that as people see the ads repeatedly, **they'll become curious about who is behind them and investigate by going to foundatchurch.com.**

After scrolling down and reading stories about what people have found at church, they will then discover the whole thing is rooted at Eagle Brook Church.

Our desire was to point people to Jesus first, then to church, then hopefully our church.

We are really excited to **watch this campaign evolve past the Easter season** and to see how our attenders continue to use this campaign to share about their church and their God on social media.

RESULTS

We had about 43,000 people at our Easter services—which spanned 42 services at six different locations. Those numbers are roughly double our normal attendance.

The original article included tons of pictures and videos we weren't able to include in this book. If you want to learn more about this campaign, see the ads Andrea and her church displayed and see a culminating report Andrea created for her church leadership, check out the original article on the Church Marketing Sucks website.

ANDREA EIKEN served as the marketing strategist at Eagle Brook Church in the Twin Cities in Minnesota for over three years. She recently transitioned into freelance design with Open Mic Studio.

Web: OpenMicStudio.net | Twitter: @AndreaAdella

EASTER STORIES
Lent Social Media

Share one cool way your church is spreading the word about Easter this year:

Social media around Easter time seems so much easier. Is that terrible to admit? Starting with the beginning of Lent we posted a daily 'Journey through Lent' that gave suggestions for changing the way you live life, such as "Fast from sarcasm" or "Let someone go ahead of you in line" or "Memorize Philippians 2:5." There were a variety of suggestions throughout the past month-and-a-half.

Jennifer Johnson is the director of communications for Sewickley Presbyterian Church in Sewickley, Penn.

HOW TO WELCOME EASTER VISITORS
by Kevin D. Hendricks

We sat down to have a conversation with Jonathan Malm about how to welcome Easter visitors. Jonathan is the author of multiple books, including *Created For More: 30 Days to Seeing Your World in a New Way* and our own *Unwelcome: 50 Ways Churches Drive Away First-Time Visitors*.

Easter is a prime time for visitors. What are some specific issues churches need to be aware of when it comes to welcoming visitors at Easter?

Jonathan Malm: I love Easter services. **They have a certain buzz about them** that you don't see in an everyday service. This comes partially from a more full service. It comes partially because **people arrive more expectant**. Where Christmas has become mostly about presents and stress, Easter is still a fairly untainted holiday. Church people realize it's about the death and resurrection of Jesus.

That creates a weird dynamic, though. Your regulars are creating one energy—confidence. While your visitors are unsure because they've either never set foot in your building or haven't been there in a year.

It's important you prepare for this hoard of lost people in your services. You need to refresh your volunteers on all their training and make sure they're ready for people who have no idea what to do at church. The first-time visitor shouldn't feel singled out. **They should feel like they're at home.**

With so many people coming to church just for Easter, how do you get them to come back?

Jonathan: I think there are two important things to realize for this question. The first is that **Easter is a chance to show people what your church is like.** Unfortunately, it's also one of the times we tend to do things we don't normally do. We have things like cantatas or dramas. A visitor coming to your church for the first time might easily think this is the norm. I wouldn't want to attend a cantata or drama each week… I'd want to attend a church. Let people know what they can expect when they come back.

Secondly, **you need to hook people to come back**. Why would someone want to come back next week? A "life-changing" event isn't one of those reasons. Most people think their lives are going just fine—otherwise they'd already be in your church. But what about something that speaks to finances, marriage or some other felt need? Nearly everyone thinks those areas of their life could be stronger. **Why not create a hook series and invite them back for it?** Connect what you have to offer in your services with what people feel like they need.

What are visitors looking for at Easter? At Christmas we understand that tradition is important, but what draws visitors to a specific church for Easter?

Jonathan: In a country that has a very strong Christian history, **there's still a tradition where people want to go to church on Easter.** It's kind of similar to liking the band U2; even if you don't really enjoy their music, you're just supposed to like U2. **It's just an expectation.**

So people are looking for a church service. They want to hear the story of Jesus, and they want to sing some songs. Meet them where they are, then delight them with something unexpected. They don't want to feel singled out, but they want to feel valued. They don't want to feel judged, but they want to hear the truth. They want you to speak their language, and they want to be able to understand.

Easter egg hunts: Harmless fun for the kids? Wonderful resurrection metaphor? Or another holiday culture clash; Jesus vs. the Easter Bunny?

Jonathan: The bottom line for kids is this: make sure they have a blast. McDonald's has taught us that parents will go where their kids drag them. **Create an amazing experience for children, and they'll want to come back.** Whether that's Easter egg hunts or bounce houses.

If you're convicted about Easter egg hunts, don't do them. But you also don't have to speak out against them. The strongest message we can send to the world is what we're for, not what we're against. **Be for fun. Be for life. Be for love.**

KEVIN D. HENDRICKS is the editor of Church Marketing Sucks and editorial director for the Center for Church Communication. He's a freelance writer and editor in St. Paul, Minn., and likes to read a lot—he wrote *137 Books in One Year: How to Fa'* *in Love With Reading.*

Web: KevinDHendricks.com
Twitter: @KevinHendricks

EASTER STORIES
Word of Mouth

Share one cool way your church is spreading the word about Easter this year:

Not by printing a lot of things that will just end up in the trash. But simply encouraging people to use word-of-mouth and invite the people in their lives.

Mark Reiswig is the ministry catalyst at Catalyst Church in Phoenix.

13 LAST MINUTE SOCIAL MEDIA IDEAS
by Steve Fogg & Erin Williams

Sometimes Easter sneaks up on you without your knowledge. You're left with no time to think of any promotional strategies, and the Easter service is upon you. Here are some quick, last-minute social media ideas to get your church noticed in the noise around Easter:

1. CREATE SHAREABLE CONTENT

As social networks increasingly create strategies requiring you to pay to reach your audience, a very smart way around their pay-wall is to equip your community with the graphic assets to share content on their own feeds. More reach with less budget. Who wouldn't want that?

2. SPEND SOME MONEY

While saving money with shareable content is a great idea, you should really invest in some paid advertising campaigns on Facebook. This year, we're running three advertisements on Facebook. Week one we posted a promotional Easter video that acted as a social "Save the Date." Week two we pinned a separate Easter video at the top of our page so the first thing people saw when they came to our page was information about our sunrise service. And week three we're re-posting a special "So God Sent His Son" video we used last year to reveal a bit of the Easter message.

3. USE VIDEO

Facebook and Twitter have launched an assault on YouTube. Facebook recently surpassed YouTube for the most desktop views per day. Expect mobile to follow soon. To increase for profit business's and nonprofit's adoption of video, Facebook seems to have taken the reach limiter off video—for the moment at least. Exploit it while you can. A video like the one mentioned above would be a great way to get people excited for Easter and will make your church stand out from the crowd.

4. GO BEHIND THE SCENES

In the lead up to Easter, one way to generate buzz is to take photos or videos of the upcoming Easter services/presentations without giving away the whole story. Give people a sneak peek.

5. GO VIRAL WITH A PHOTO BOOTH

We've done photo booths for our major outreach services, and it's a great way to reach more people in a very family-friendly way.

6. KEEP YOUR SOCIAL FEED UP TO DATE

Are old sermon series headlining your platforms? Make sure your branding is on time and doesn't hang around too long so it becomes out of date. As we approach Easter, you should have Easter info dominating your social feed.

We talked about the simple idea of putting Easter service times on your website. Do the same for social. On both Twitter and Facebook, you can "pin" a post to the top to make sure it's always the first thing people see. Pin your Easter info to the top of your profile.

You can also use Easter graphics as your cover photos on Twitter and Facebook and profile links on Twitter and Instagram instead of your church logo. This simple tweak says, "Easter's a big deal; there's nothing more important for us to tell you about."

7. SHARE STORIES

Some of our church's best program promotion across the board has been through sharing stories. How has such-and-such class improved your understanding of the Bible? What difference have our sermons made in your life? When people can connect what's happening in church to real life and then share that, you've got a powerful advertisement. This year, some of our staff members have written relevant, Easter-themed stories and shared them on both our church's and their own personal social platforms.

8. CELEBRATE YOUR VOLUNTEERS

Your church is more than just a building. Your church is all about people, and many of those people serve faithfully. Why not celebrate your volunteers? By tagging them on your Facebook, Twitter or Instagram posts, you also tell their friends that your church appreciates them. Oh, and your church is also now in their friends' feed. That's pretty cool free exposure.

9. CREATE STICKY QUOTE PHOTOS

Have content generators on hand throughout the Easter weekend. You can capture the insightful sticky phrase from your pastors. A photographer can take some photos of your speaker(s). Your designer can create a quotable quote graphic. Put them up on your social feeds after the services. The insights that resonated with the audience at the time are very shareable and will spread through your community's social networks.

10. CREATE A HASHTAG

Create a fun hashtag and promote it in your services and your communication channels in the days leading up to your Easter services. Something like #EatMoreEggs or #ThereIsNoSuchThingAsTooMuchChocolate or #HamOrLamb. You get the idea. It doesn't have to be super spiritual. It's simply about finding a fun way to engage people. (Pro tip: Initial cap your hashtags so they're easier to read.)

11. CREATE A THUNDERCLAP

Create a social media message and a compelling photo to share with the Thunderclap service. Email your congregation and ask them to lend their voice to the post. This is a great way to get a message out at a certain time.

12. BUILD A VOLUNTEER SOCIAL MEDIA TEAM

Easter is a busy enough time. Ask around to see who is interested in photography or helping out on social media. Look at your feeds and see who is on there all the time. This is a great way to identify potential volunteers.

13. INVITE PEOPLE PERSONALLY

Smiling faces might be your best advertisement. Last year, we invited people by taking pictures of our staff members holding a board that said, "Come with me to church on Easter!" This year, we stepped our invitations up a notch and had them share their favorite part about Easter on video and then invite people to church. These videos were posted on Twitter, Instagram and Facebook.

STEVE FOGG serves as the big cheese of communications at his church in Melbourne, Australia; he married way above his pay grade and has three children. Connect with him on his blog or on other social networks.

Web: SteveFogg.com | Twitter: @SteveFogg

ERIN WILLIAMS is a writer and editor for RightNow Media and a blogger for Amanda and Erin Ministry. She lives in a fun yellow house in Dallas and enjoys family, friendship, food and wine, fitness, coffee and ranches.

Web: AmandaAndErin.com | Twitter: @ewilliams5242

EASTER STORIES
Facebook Promotion

Share one cool way your church is spreading the word about Easter this year:

Our contemporary worship service is just two years old but very active, thanks in large part to Facebook. It was and remains our primary advertising machine. From the weeks prior to the service launching, we spent a few hundred dollars to drive interest and invite a few folks to check out the page/service. In a matter of months, we had as many followers as our parent church. Over the years, we have never spent money on ads, leaning instead on organic reach.

However, for this year's Easter week, we threw a mere $200 at our Facebook campaign. We boosted several posts to those who liked the page and their friends. These posts included word quote images (our favorite apps are WordSwag, Over and InstaQuote), linked content (articles that explained Maundy Thursday, Good Friday, etc.), iPhone videos from the pastor as she was prepping for the sermons, the band's first music video and—of course—invitations to join us for the many worship opportunities.

It worked.

We reached over 28,000 people during the week, with 55 new page likes, over 600 total likes and 74 shares (that's huge), and our videos reached over 10,000 people, almost half of whom actually viewed the videos. By analyzing the Facebook analytics (which is just cool), we were able to see that much of the spike in activity was thanks to advertising. But keep in mind, we didn't spend a ton of money—$200 for the entire week, $5 here, $10 there. All of this is testament that, in the Facebook world, spending just a few dollars to boost posts pays off. For the smaller churches, just spending $10 will—and in our case—did yield a huge result.

The larger question one would, and should, ask is, "did it result in greater attendance?" We've always maintained that the online audience is just as important as the audience who attends, so that question is somewhat misleading. But yes, there were more people than last year. In fact, there were three times as many people. In hindsight, we would have loved to have cross-checked how many of the newcomers were a result of our increased Facebook marketing, but at the end of the day, sharing the message becomes the most important deliverable.

Todd Rossnagel is a lay leader at First United Methodist Church in Baton Rouge, La.

BEAT THE STRESS

3 SIMPLE TO-DOS FOR A BETTER EASTER
by Kevin D. Hendricks

On Palm Sunday, we remember Christ's triumphant march into Jerusalem with waving palm branches. And so marks the beginning of the inevitable march to Easter, your last-minute, last-ditch effort to get everything done during Holy Week and before Easter Sunday. It can be a crazy week for church communicators, and honestly, it's too late to launch anything new. So we've got three simple things to help you out this final week: Prayer, Peace & Post Personally.

1. PRAYER

First and foremost, this is a good time to pray. One of the first things West Ridge Church communications director Phil Bowdle mentioned when talking about Easter during our podcast was prayer:

"We're focusing a lot on prayer. We often get so wrapped up in our own plans and ideas, and 'here's how we want it to go.' But we know nothing of eternal significance happens apart from prayer. So for us, even as a team, we're trying to focus on that side of it too, and pray that God will use Easter services here and all over in a big way."

Spend this week praying that God would bring visitors to your Easter services. Pray for God to move and people to respond. Pray that lives would be changed by the greatest story ever told. This is why we do what we do.

2. PEACE

If you work in the church, Easter can be crazy. There's last-minute promotion, big Sunday morning production and lots of pressure not to disappoint.

That's all true, but take a breath. There's a point where we just need to let it go. Easter shouldn't be about pressure and stress. Take a page from Lutheran pastor Nadia Bolz-Weber, who contends that "the God of Easter is a God with dirt under his nails":

"For many churches Easter is basically another word for church showoff day—a time when we spiff up the building, pull out the lilies, hire a brass quintet, and put on fabulous hats and do whatever we have to do to impress visitors. To me, it had always felt kind of like the church's version of putting out the guest towels, which makes no sense. Easter is not a story about new dresses and flowers and spiffiness. Really, it's a story about flesh and dirt and bodies and confusion, and it's about the way God never seems to adhere to our expectations of what a proper God would do (as in not get himself killed in a totally avoidable way).

"Jesus didn't look very impressive at Easter, not in the churchy sense, and certainly not if Mary Magdalene mistook him for a gardener.

"… It happens to all of us. God simply keeps reaching down into the dirt of humanity and resurrecting us from the graves we dig for ourselves through our violence, our lies, our selfishness, our arrogance, and our addictions. And God keeps loving us back to life over and over." (*Pastrix: The Cranky, Beautiful Faith of a Sinner & Saint*)

You may not completely buy in to Bolz-Weber's anti-excellence perspective, but that's OK. Let the pressure go this week and focus on how Easter is about God making all things new.

3. POST PERSONALLY

The simplest thing you can do to share your church's Easter experience with your wider community is to post personally. Take a picture, shoot a video, jot down a quote. Some of you will be doing that anyway in some official capacity as the official tweeter for your church. But do it for yourself. Do it personally, on your personal account. Share the stories that matter to you. Take a picture of your view. Share your Easter experience with people who aren't sitting next to you in the pew.

Sometimes as communicators everything we do is professional promotion. That can get old. And we can start to forget why we're there in the first place. But if we're simply present and part of the experience, we can share it more naturally. We can rediscover authenticity.

Take a moment this Easter to step back from your official duties and post as yourself.

Here's to a great Easter experience at your church. We pray people will respond to the gospel. We hope you will find peace in your preparation. And we look forward to seeing personal posts about your Easter.

KEVIN D. HENDRICKS is the editor of Church Marketing Sucks and editorial director for the Center for Church Communication. He's a freelance writer and editor in St. Paul, Minn., and likes to read a lot—he wrote *137 Books in One Year: How to Fall in Love With Reading.*

Web: KevinDHendricks.com | Twitter: @KevinHendricks

EASTER STORIES
Teamwork

How do you keep your focus on the joy of Easter amid the stress of looming deadlines and long hours?

We laughed a lot as a team! We collaborated on all of the creative elements and shared tasks, so no one person carried all the burden. We intentionally took time to have lunch together one week out. We stopped and prayed together for Easter services. We shared stories of the people we were inviting. We ate donuts.

Christine Pitt is the communication/creative director at Valley Creek Church in Flower Mound, Texas.

YOU RECHARGE YOUR PHONE, HOW ABOUT YOUR SOUL?
by Adam Legg

"Happiness is not a matter of intensity but of balance, order, rhythm and harmony." -Thomas Merton

We live in a creation that is full of rhythm.

Winter, spring, summer, fall.

Sunrise and sunset.

Planting and harvest.

The rising and falling of the tides.

We even get a glimpse of God's rhythm at the very beginning of these natural cycles in Genesis 1 when God works and rests.

Consider that the very first gift God gave to mankind was rest. Adam and Eve's first experience in creation and with their creator was to rest and enjoy what he had created.

Yet too often we forget that we, as created beings, are in need of rhythm in our own lives. Especially as we approach Easter and are tempted to push off rest and sanity until Holy Week is behind us.

THE GIFT OF RHYTHM

"I am the vine, you are the branches. Those who abide in me and I in them bear much fruit, because apart from me you can do nothing." -John 15:5

Did you notice what our role is in this verse? To produce? Hustle? Strive? To live out of rhythm? No.

To abide.

When our producing consumes our abiding we adopt an unsustainable pace that robs us of the gift in the rhythms God gave us.

Work hard? Absolutely!

Dream big and work toward that? Certainly!

But when those things become the driving force of our lives we are in trouble. Our source of inspiration fades, dreaming becomes a task and creation seems duty-bound.

How is the rhythm in your own life? Do you feel tired, burned out, exhausted, ready for a break, constantly needing a vacation? Has your inspiration, dreaming and creating become exhausting rather than life giving?

Your life rhythm may be off and in need of realigning.

WHAT DO YOU DO WHEN YOU REALIZE YOUR RHYTHM IS OFF?

I've recently set some goals for myself when I start drowning in my work and realize I need to take a step away to save myself (and my work):

- **Get Away:** It doesn't have to be two weeks on some remote beach (although if that's possible, do it!). Sometimes it just takes a weekend at a lake or a local B&B to return to a healthy rhythm. It might be too late to fit that in before Easter this year. That's OK. Recognize you need it and plan ahead for next year.
- **Unplug:** The average cell phone user in America checks their phone 150 times a day. Take a day where you turn your phone off and unplug. Read an actual book. Play a board game. Eat a meal and don't Instagram a photo of it! Just

unplug from electronics, and plug into something that is life giving.

- **Get Inspired:** As creative people, we are often renewed through creative inspiration. In 2011, when my life rhythm was horribly wrong, I went to the Echo Conference. Even though it was a busy few days with lots of things going on, I found rest and abiding because of how inspiring the environment was for me. Look for a conference or workshop that gets you excited, not wears you out.
- **Get Out:** Go for a walk, take a hike, climb a mountain, go fishing, fly a kite, feed the birds. Do anything that gets you out of an office or a coffee shop and into nature. There is something incredibly peaceful about being alone in creation where our rhythms originally began.
- **Connect to the Vine:** Too often we try and do God's work in our power. Be intentional about your personal time with God. Make it a priority and allow God's peace and rest to permeate your time. Often when we've reached the point of exhaustion, he's beckoning us to just be still and rest in him.

HOW DO YOU KEEP YOURSELF IN RHYTHM?

Maybe you aren't experiencing unhealthy rhythm in your life right now, but we still need to guard against that temptation. These are ways I am learning to become a warrior of my rest and guard against my work robbing me of healthy rhythms:

- **One Day:** In the Old Testament, God was constantly reminding his people to keep the Sabbath holy. I'm not suggesting we be bound to the law, but there is great significance in God wanting his people to remember and take time to enjoy his first gift to mankind—rest. Over and over again, God promises to give his people rest. Take one day (for some of us it can't be Sunday) that isn't devoted to work and truly rest.
- **Guard Your Mind:** Your moments are sacred. It's sacred to honor your covenant relationship with the Lord, your spouse, your family, your spiritual partners. But too often that is when we begin remembering the list of things we have to do at work. I drive in my car with the windows

down, and the ideas and tasks begin piling up. I have to vigilantly guard my mind against the list of things I have to do. If I am inspired by something on my day off, I write it down and forget it until my next workday.

- **Infuse With Life:** Your days and times of rest need to be life giving. These are the opportunities you get to take time to breathe and refocus. So don't schedule a coffee with someone who will drag you down. Don't change the tires on your car if you know that's a battle. Don't do things that cause you stress. These are the moments necessary to infuse life back into you and into your work.

- **Moments Matter:** Moments throughout the day matter, and sometimes you may just need a moment. If you find yourself pressed against a figurative wall or meeting a roadblock, take a moment. Stand up and stretch. Flip through a coffee table book. Close your eyes for a minute. Find a moment to do something that inspires you or gives you a chance to breathe. Rest in that moment and enjoy it.

Remember, when we become people who press into producing, rather than press into abiding, we take on the unnecessary burden of producing fruit in our life, instead of allowing God to do that, and we begin to live a rhythm that we were never created to sustain.

We rob him of the gift he intended for us—a gift that for us as creatives is imperative to making inspired work. Without rest we begin producing rather than creating.

Stop. Breathe. Listen.

What is God saying to you about the rhythm in your life as you approach Easter?

ADAM LEGG is the creative arts and communications pastor at ChangePoint in Anchorage, Alaska, a regular blogger at www.adamlegg.com and can be found on Twitter. He enjoys travel, art, music and sports, and he's pretty sure YouTube is the greatest invention ever.

Web: AdamLegg.com | Twitter: @AdamLegg

EASTER STORIES
Start Early

How do you keep your focus on the joy of Easter amid the stress of looming deadlines and long hours?

It can get really overwhelming at times, but our approach is to start early, prioritize, assign specific tasks with timelines and hold regular meetings to communicate updates.

Damilola Okuneye leads the media team at Church 3:16 in Lagos, Nigeria.

EASTER IS OVER, NOW WHAT?
by Kelvin Co

What do you do when Easter is over? When the biggest event of the year in the church world is behind us, what's next? Before moving on to the next big event (or the next Sunday service for that matter), consider the following:

CELEBRATE

How was Easter at your church? Attendance was probably high. A lot of people probably got saved. Capture the information and stories and celebrate! Share the wins with staff and volunteers. Celebrate it with your congregation the next Sunday. Champion the volunteers and staff who went above and beyond to serve the large crowds. Brag on the people working behind-the-scenes on social media. Write thank you notes.

EVALUATE

One thing is for sure: Easter will happen again next year. While the experience is fresh, start planning now by asking key questions. What went well? What should we keep doing? What went wrong? What should we stop doing? Capture key numbers like attendance, first-time guests, salvations, etc. Then tee yourself for next year by setting up a reminder to look at this information when you start planning for next Easter.

RESET

There's an expression, "The project is not done until the tools have been put away." Have the props from the Easter special been put away? Have the leftover invite cards been recycled? Has all the Easter promo stuff been removed from the website? Being intentional about this step creates a culture of thoroughness and excellence. Sloppiness erodes your credibility and compromises the power of a successful event.

RECHARGE

Easter was a lot of work! Before diving into your next big thing (Mother's Day, Father's Day, summer events, fall, Christmas, etc.) make sure to rest, dote on your family and soak in God's Word and presence for a fresh revelation.

KELVIN CO gets to do what he loves as the creative arts pastor of The Oaks Fellowship located in the Dallas Metroplex area. Kelvin has been doing life together with his wife and best friend Lucy since 1991, and they have been doting on and pouring into their son Luc since 2002.

Web: KelvinCo.com | Twitter: @KelvinCo

EASTER STORIES
Connect With Coworkers

How do you keep your focus on the joy of Easter amid the stress of looming deadlines and long hours?

I don't always—I often find myself distracted and disheartened by the mighty to-do list. But when I see that I've gotten off track and my stress level is high, I try to take a step back, pray and talk with my coworkers who are dealing with the same thing.

Jared Brandon is the director of communications at Parker Hill Church in Scranton, Pa.

SCRIPTURE THAT RECHARGES THE SOUL
by Erin Williams

In our #cmschat on Twitter, our host Steve Fogg asked how we're caring for ourselves spiritually and then asked for "a Scripture that recharges our soul."

Why ask for a verse? "It's easy for us to get lost in our work rather than in who we worship," Steve said.

Lots of people chimed in with Bible verses that encouraged and inspired them in the midst of the challenges of preparing for Easter. So we collected those inspiring Bible verses in one place. Maybe one will jump out and recharge your soul today:

- "Make a careful exploration of who you are and the work you have been given, and then sink yourself into that. Don't be impressed with yourself. Don't compare yourself with others. Each of you must take responsibility for doing the creative best you can with your own life." -Galatians 6:4-5, The Message (Shayla Kenworthy)
- "For if you remain silent at this time, relief and deliverance for the Jews will arise from another place, but you and your father's family will perish. And who knows but that you have come to your royal position for such a time as this?" -Esther 4:14, NIV (Mark David Johnson)
- "Come to me, all you who are weary and burdened, and I will give you rest. Take my yoke upon you and learn from me, for I am gentle and humble in heart, and you will find rest for your souls. For my yoke is easy and my burden is light." -Matthew 11:28-30, NIV (Steve Fogg)

- "'For I know the plans I have for you,' declares the Lord, 'plans to prosper you and not to harm you, plans to give you hope and a future.'" -Jeremiah 29:11, NIV (Ta Quinda Marie)
- "This is what the LORD says to Israel: 'Seek me and live.'" -Amos 5:4, NIV (Emily Bedwell)
- "As you enter the house of God, keep your ears open and your mouth shut. It is evil to make mindless offerings to God. Don't make rash promises, and don't be hasty in bringing matters before God. After all, God is in heaven, and you are here on earth. So let your words be few. Too much activity gives you restless dreams; too many words make you a fool." -Ecclesiastes 5:1-3, NLT (Neal Fischer)
- "Jesus got up, rebuked the wind and said to the waves, 'Quiet! Be still!' Then the wind died down and it was completely calm." -Mark 4:39, NIV (Tim Sheare)
- "Your love has given me great joy and encouragement, because you, brother, have refreshed the hearts of the Lord's people." -Philemon 1:7, NIV (Shayla Kenworthy)
- "Oh, how abundant is your goodness, which you have stored up for those who fear you and worked for those who take refuge in you, in the sight of the children of mankind!" -Psalm 31:19, ESV (Jared Callais)
- "See, I am doing a new thing! Now it springs up; do you not perceive it? I am making a way in the wilderness and streams in the wasteland." -Isaiah 43:19, NIV (Anthony Stone)
- "I'm asking God for one thing, only one thing: To live with him in his house my whole life long." -Psalm 27:4, The Message (Gin Hannen)

Church communication can be hard, especially before and after our biggest days of the year. Take care of yourself and don't forget to stay rooted in the message we're trying to communicate.

We hope you find the encouragement, restoration and care your soul needs for the work you do.

ERIN WILLIAMS is a writer and editor for RightNow Media and a blogger for Amanda and Erin Ministry. She lives in a fun yellow house in Dallas and enjoys family, friendship, food and wine, fitness, coffee and ranches.

Web: AmandaAndErin.com | Twitter: @ewilliams5242

EASTER STORIES
Prayer

How do you keep your focus on the joy of Easter amid the stress of looming deadlines and long hours?

Easter is always stressful, and this year was no different. I know it sounds cliche, but prayer makes a huge difference. Pressing into prayer and time alone with God helps take the edge off.

Bryan Baker is the lead pastor at Big Timber Evangelical Church in Big Timber, Mont.

AN EASTER PRAYER FOR CHURCH COMMUNICATORS

Father, we come to you now, and we are grateful for the opportunity you have given us and that you have entrusted us as your servants to help communicate your truth. It's a powerful message. And the same power that raised Christ from the dead is in us and in those who will be coming to experience and celebrate the Easter resurrection morning.

We pray for the teams, the communication teams, those who are designing the graphics, those who are—even now—trying to find those answers they need in order to prepare for this great celebration on Easter. We pray that you will give them strength, you will give them wisdom, you will give them the courage they need to raise up and bring those conversations that need to happen to the forefront.

And we pray that you will work in a powerful way in all of these worship services across world, Father, that your name will be honored and glorified in all that is done.

In Jesus' name we pray, Amen.

-Gerry True

MORE

ABOUT THE CENTER FOR CHURCH COMMUNICATION

We are a firebrand of communicators, sparking churches to communicate the gospel clearly, effectively and without compromise.

We are made up of passionate change agents, experienced communication professionals and thoughtful instigators; advocating for communicators to find their place in the church—and helping the church get through to their communities so that churches know who they are and are unashamed to tell others.

We identify, resource and celebrate the next generation of church communicators, encouraging them to focus their tenacity and talent for excellent communication, so that churches are sought out by the communities they serve.

We provide smart coaching and mentoring through social media, publishing, events and one-on-one relationships, spotlighting communication that is true, good and beautiful—prompting others to do the same—so that more outsiders become a part of a church community.

We remove barriers to change the way people see Christians and how they speak about the church by promoting relationships, resources, ideas and models for communication. We collaborate people's gifts/skills to work in concert with the Creator and their local church.

As God's story comes alive to us and others, we see gospel-centered local churches that captivate the attention and liberate the imagination of their community, resulting in more people saying, "That's what church should be!"

Center for Church Communication:
Courageous storytellers welcome.

Visit CFCCLabs.org to learn more about our projects and get involved.

For more practical tips, inspiration and stories from fellow communicators, visit our flagship blog, Church Marketing Sucks.

MORE CHURCH COMMUNICATION HELP

You need all the help you can get when planning for holidays. Check out these other books from the Center for Church Communication to get more ideas and inspiration:

Church Easter Ideas
Find even more ideas, examples and Easter resources for churches at Church Marketing Sucks.

God Rest Ye Stressed Church Communicators: Planning Christmas for Your Church
Christmas isn't always a season of peace on earth and goodwill toward men, especially for communicators. Save the stress this season with Christmas tips from more than a dozen church communication pros.

Go to cfcclabs.org/christmas to purchase this book.

Unwelcome: 50 Ways Churches Drive Away First-Time Visitors
Jonathan Malm talks about how churches drive away visitors and gives advice for keeping them in the pews.

Go to UnwelcomeBook.com to purchase this book.

FREE SOCIAL MEDIA GRAPHICS

A picture is worth a thousand words (which is great when it comes to promoting your Easter series or event). So we're giving you some for free. Use these Easter graphics to share the hope of the resurrection on social media.

Download the free graphics here: http://cmsucks.us/acc

If you don't like this graphic, you can always create your own. *The Church Graphics Handbook* has plenty of tips and help.

We hope either of these options helps you with your Easter series or event. Happy planning!

ACKNOWLEDGEMENTS

Thanks to our contributors: Phil Bowdle, Kelvin Co, Evan Courtney, Andrea Eiken, Steve Fogg, Kelly Hartnett, Kevin D. Hendricks, Adam Legg, Angie Shoaf, Gerry True and Erin Williams.

Thanks for the stories: Bryan Baker, Jared Brandon, Carrie Evans, Jennifer Johnson, Tom Lelyo, Michelle Mumm, Santosh Ninan, Damilola Okuneye, Christine Pitt, Mark Reiswig and Todd Rossnagel.

Kevin D. Hendricks for seeing this project through.

Elizabyth Ladwig for getting this project started.

Laura Bennett for the cover and interior design.

Chuck Scoggins for leading the Center for Church Communication through these projects.

Katie Strandlund for creating a marketing plan and keeping us organized.

Thanks to those who helped proof this book: Erin Williams and Robert Carnes. You made sure we placed all our commas in the right places.

Thank you to everyone reading this book. We hope it helps you in your efforts to make your church's Easter celebrations more organized, creative and meaningful. As an added bonus, your purchase supports the work of the Center for Church Communication to help churches communicate better. If you found this book valuable, we hope you'll spread the word.

Made in the USA
San Bernardino, CA
27 February 2018